The Library of
E-Commerce and Internet Careers

Careers in E-Commerce Software Development

Jason T. Roff and
Kimberly A. Roff

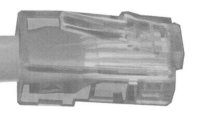

The Rosen Publishing Group, Inc.
New York

Published in 2001 by The Rosen Publishing Group, Inc.
29 East 21st Street, New York, NY 10010

Library of Congress Cataloging-in-Publication Data

Roff, Jason T.
Careers in e-commerce software development / by Jason T. and
Kimberly A. Roff.
p. cm. — (The library of e-commerce and Internet careers)
Includes bibliographical references and index.
ISBN 0-8239-3421-7
1. Computer software—Development—Vocational guidance—
Juvenile literature. [1. Computer software industry—Vocational
guidance. 2. Vocational guidance.]
I. Roff, Kimberly A. II. Title. III. Series.
QA76.76.D47 R647 2001
005.1'023'73—dc21

2001001043

Manufactured in the United States of America

Table of Contents

Introduction

More than ever, America needs software developers. In fact, America's demand for software developers is so great that it has recently raised the maximum number of work visas it grants per year. The number of foreign software developers who come from overseas to work in the United States has increased from 115,000 to an estimated 400,000 by 2002. Still, this is not enough to meet the constant demand. According to the U.S. Bureau of Labor Statistics, opportunities in computer engineering are among the top three fastest growing career choices right now.

Some of the benefits of this growth are demonstrated by the salary increases in this field. While most jobs are paying modest salary increases that average around 4 percent, software developers will see average salary increases of 14 percent. What does this mean to you? It means simply this: There has never been a better time to enter the job market if you are a software developer.

Marshall Harrison, president of Imperium Solutions, wants to hire more employees but is having a difficult time finding well-trained software developers.

Being a software developer, or programmer—the terms are somewhat interchangeable—requires a certain type of person, a certain type of exposure, and a great deal of knowledge about a rapidly changing field. But if you don't know how to use a computer, you won't be able to program for one. Start by learning the common programs for the computers you are using in school, such as basic word-processing software and spreadsheets. Also, one of the most basic concepts that you need to understand right from the start is that a computer will never do something it is not told to do. Humans program computers. Humans tell computers what to do, right or wrong. Understanding this concept will take you a long way.

Software developers who are designing for the purposes of e-commerce—buying and selling goods online—have a host of additional needs to consider, outside of programming basics. E-commerce software developers must think about programming their designs with high-tech security measures. For instance, a program that is designed to record credit card information must be able to encrypt that information, or scramble it, so that others cannot view it as it is stored on an e-tailer's electronic online server. This same program might be required to have a "shopping cart" function, enabling a customer to browse and save information about items he or she would like to purchase, or to have the ability to sort data for the purposes of marketing. Also, the software must be programmed to accept payments, calculate shipping costs, and even anticipate the needs of repeat customers! A well-designed e-commerce software program will have the ability to do all of these things and more.

Who Are Software Developers?

Software developers are no longer considered to be computer geeks. Almost anyone with a willingness to learn and the persistence to practice computer skills can become a successful e-commerce software developer.

WHO DEVELOPS SOFTWARE?

It takes a very analytical person to be a software developer. Having the ability to solve problems logically is essential. Many people claim that being good at math is very important—and in a way it is—but it is not entirely necessary. By nature, people who are good at math are also excellent problem solvers. They are able to solve problems logically, just as you must be able to do when you develop software. However, it is possible to be good at solving problems logically without necessarily being good at math.

TYPES OF SOFTWARE DEVELOPERS

Today there are many types of software developers. Some develop for the Web, while others develop software for personal computers (PCs) that run Windows, Linux, MacOs, BeOS, or a number of other operating systems. There are software developers who write source code (computer programs) for cars, refrigerators, smoke detectors, coffee pots, and just about anything else that utilizes a circuit board. Source code is a set of instructions that is created by programmers to tell a computer how to do its work. Then the source code is compiled into a binary, or computer-readable, file. A binary system is one that contains only two choices: numbers that consist only of a series of 1s and 0s.

With the growth of the Internet, software developers' jobs are changing rapidly. In today's field, somebody who has only two years of training in a particular technology can be considered well-experienced, and may be sought after for many positions.

Because of the current and projected future demand, software developers enjoy a very good salary in today's economy. Top-level developers are currently accustomed to large salary increases, signing bonuses, and, in many situations, other perks most professions would never offer. The average entry-level salary for a computer programmer in an urban area is $54,000 a year, but, of course, salaries are based upon experience, knowledge, and your willingness to work hard.

THE WORK ENVIRONMENT

Over the last few years, developers have been expected to work harder than usual to meet the demand for new and better software. It is not unheard of to work an eighty-hour work week that encompasses both weekends and nights. This has been normal for many Internet startup companies that have been struggling to make enough profit to become stable, successful businesses. Dot-com start-up companies sometimes offer unusual perks to their workers, such as in-house chefs, massages, and even pet care. In return, you have to be willing to give them everything you've got! For these reasons, working for a startup has become very popular among younger developers. They have less to lose if the company fails, but they also have the potential to earn tremendous amounts of money if the company goes public (openly traded on the stock market).

As a software developer, you may find yourself spending long hours investigating technical difficulties and solving software problems.

As one of the perks granted in exchange for working hard, many Internet startup companies offer stock options before the company goes public. This stock might be inexpensively sold to employees, or even given to them for free, as a work-related incentive. For example, if a company goes public, thousands of shares of stock that cost an employee ten cents each could skyrocket and be worth hundreds of dollars each in only a matter of weeks. Of course, as more and more dot-com startups enter the public arena, the possibility of this type of financial reward is becoming rare. Now, the few jobs where employees become millionaires are as hard to come by as winning the lottery!

Fortune 500 companies—businesses with a high earning potential as defined by *Fortune* magazine— are well established. Most offer excellent security for software developers and good benefits, such as insurance and vacation time. In addition, you would be more likely to work a forty-hour week for a larger, established company than you would for a smaller company that has recently entered the market. Lately, employees seem divided about which type of employment offers the most appealing benefits.

As a software developer, the work environment that you seek is going to depend on several factors, including annual earnings, bonuses, and other perks, as well as considerations such as office space, work environment, and co-workers. For instance, some people enjoy wearing a suit and a tie everyday and want to work for a large, secure company such as IBM, while others like to roll out of bed and go to work in sweats. There is probably no other profession that has as many lifestyle variables as do careers in the field of software development. Take your pick.

FULL-TIME OR CONSULTING DEVELOPERS

There are two types of developers: full-time employees and freelance consultants. Full-time employees usually enjoy benefits such as health insurance, a 401K (retirement) plan with company matching, paid vacation time, and sick leave. A freelance consultant, on the other hand, gets paid by the hour, usually without any of these benefits. The advantage for the freelance consultant is that his or her hourly rate is usually much higher than that of a full-time employee.

Because freelance consultants have to pay for their own health insurance, and have to save for the times when they are not working (either in between projects or when they want to take a vacation or sick day), their pay is higher. A salaried employee can enjoy the benefit of not having to take out money from each paycheck to put toward federal and state taxes and social security, but a consultant receives all of the money that he or she has earned immediately. Later, however, he or she is responsible for paying taxes— either every quarter or once a year. This means that if a freelance consultant made $100,000 in one year, he or she could potentially owe the government $35,000 by tax day, April 15. This could be a major problem if he or she isn't good with money and didn't sock away the needed cash after each paycheck.

If you are careful with money, and don't mind working for many different people over short periods of time, you might enjoy working as a freelance consultant. Freelancers can enjoy many more tax breaks than regular employees can, because, in essence, a freelance consultant is running his or her own business, whereas an employee works for a business that has its own tax deductions. For instance, a consul-

> "The best way to prepare to be a programmer is to write programs, and to study great programs that other people have written. In my case, I went to the garbage cans at the computer science center and fished out listings of their operating system."
>
> **—Bill Gates**

tant can usually "write off" (subtract work-related expenses from the tax money he or she owes) computer equipment, transportation costs, clothing, telephone bills, and almost anything else associated with working. What this means is, if you can get enough tax write-offs, you can reduce the amount of income that the government taxes. A salaried employee does not have this option.

Before you get your hopes up and decide that you want to jump into freelance consulting, you must realize what a client will expect from you. A freelance consultant is usually considered an expert in his or her field. It is not unusual for a consultant to be highly specialized in one particular technology, such as database development, or graphical user interface (GUI) design. For some newer technologies, you can become an expert in as little as six months or a year, but for other technologies that have been around for a while, such as C++, you most likely won't be able to consult with only a year of experience. In contrast, regular full-time work can really pay off since a company will be more willing to train a software developer than a client would a freelance consultant. An established company can invest a great deal of money in your future if you are willing to learn and grow as a developer with that company.

In today's Internet technology (IT) workplace, there are places for all types of people. Lately, software developers can call the shots because companies need more developers than are available. This is what is known as demand in the job market. Because the demand for developers is so great, compensation for jobs related to development are high. You may choose to work for a company, or you may decide to switch to freelance consulting.

Types of Software Development

Before you decide to become a software developer, you must understand several basic ideas. There are many ways that you can improve your computer programming skills while you are still in school. Today, software packages are available that allow you to write simple computer programs. One example of this is called Visual Studio, which is available from Microsoft. Visual Studio allows you to work in any of several different computer languages including C++, Java, Visual Basic, FoxPro, and Visual InterDev. The benefit of using this type of programming software is that it offers all the tools that a computer programmer relies upon to do his or her work. For example, Visual Basic includes an integrated editor (a program for writing source code and saving it to a file), a debugger (a tool that allows you to find mistakes in the program that you wrote), and a compiler (a program that translates source code into machine language).

Understand that although it is possible to learn what you need to know without having to complete college and earn a four-year computer science degree, a college education does not lack value in the computer software industry.

There are three choices that you should make when deciding which type of software development career you want to pursue. First, you must choose what types of operating systems you want to develop for. Second, you must choose what types of hardware you want to develop for. Finally, you must choose which languages you want to develop in. Of course, you may want to branch out and learn more as your career progresses, but you must have a place to start. For example, you may first want to learn programming for Windows-only operating systems.

OPERATING SYSTEMS AND HARDWARE

There are many types of operating systems, including UNIX, Linux, and Windows. Let's begin with the world's most common operating system, Windows. Developed by Microsoft, Windows has grown into a family of products that may include not only your home computer but also devices such as palm computers, gaming devices, and car stereo systems.

The most common Windows operating systems are Windows 95, Windows 98, Windows NT, and Windows 2000. These systems run on Intel-based personal computers. Each functions similarly and can usually be developed with the same programming or code base. Another operating system that Microsoft has introduced is Windows CE. It is often used in devices such as personal computers, hand-held computers, car stereos, and the most popular gaming devices.

Apple Computer developed a popular operating system called MacOS. Educational facilities and creative professionals such as writers, artists, publishers, and video and Web producers have traditionally used MacOS. The MacOS is an elegant operating system that focuses on rich media—graphics, video animation, and audio.

Linux is another popular operating system, especially for developers who are designing software for the purposes of e-commerce. Linux is a free version of the common UNIX operating system. (UNIX is usually found on higher-end machines than those used for Windows operating systems.) Linux, however, is a very lightweight, flexible, stable, and free version of the popular operating system, and can run on nearly

Software Spotlight: Red Hat, Inc.

An e-commerce success story that utilizes the Linux open-ended operating system is Red Hat, Inc., a company that began offering software solutions to customers in 1995. With the combined efforts of owners Marc Ewing and Bob Young, who together had more than twenty years of experience in software development, Red Hat began offering pure source code to other companies. This computer code would tailor the programs to fit their exact e-commerce needs. In short, Red Hat offers computer professionals a chance to create their own e-commerce software based on the secure and flexible Linux operating system. According to Paul McNamara, general manager of Red Hat's enterprise business unit, "Red Hat is like a trusted guide. We take this enormous body of information that is Linux and turn it into something useful for customers."

The Internet virtually revolutionized the dynamics of how and in what quantity information is available to the public. Now the use of open-source software could have a dramatic effect on small businesses entering the e-commerce marketplace. Red Hat predicts that open-source software will fundamentally change the entire software industry.

anything with a microprocessor. Linux has been ported (translated) to personal computers, as well as hand-held devices, car stereos, MP3 players, and home appliances. The lure of both Linux and UNIX is that they are very secure and are the preferred operating systems of small Internet servers. This is one of the reasons why they are commonly found on Web servers that feed the Internet with information.

Magic eMerchant is a specific example of e-commerce software that utilizes the open-source (not limited to one manufacturer) Linux operating system. Because Linux developed Magic eMerchant, it may be used by any individual, no matter what type of computer he or she has. Magic eMerchant features many special features. Some tools allow e-tailers to store customer orders, while others make suggestions to customers based upon stored data, such as the availability and inventory of goods, or upon a customer's past buying history. Does any of this sound familiar? It should. Amazon.com has been using this type of programming technology since its inception, and has become one of the most successful models in the world of e-commerce properties.

Another available operating system is BeOS by Be, Inc. BeOS is also focused on supplying graphics and media and offering excellent performance for your personal computer.

LANGUAGES

After you have chosen one or several operating systems to work with, you should also choose a language to program in. There are many languages available today, but some of the most popular include Visual Basic, C and C++, Java, and Assembler. You may also want to learn Internet scripting (HTML, DHTML, and JavaScript). The languages that you choose to program in reflect the types of software that you will eventually develop. For instance, C++ is often the choice for commercial software developers.

Visual Basic

Visual Basic was developed by Microsoft and is currently available only for Windows operating systems. Visual Basic, or VB for short, is an excellent starter language and a good one to use for complex software development. Visual Basic is a simple language that is object-oriented and scalable. (Object-oriented means that the language allows the developer to represent things as objects that can be easily manipulated. Scalable means that the language can be used to develop a small application that can later be expanded over a network such as the Internet.) Visual Basic has been around for about ten years and is based on an older language named BASIC, or Beginner's All-purpose Symbolic Instruction Code.

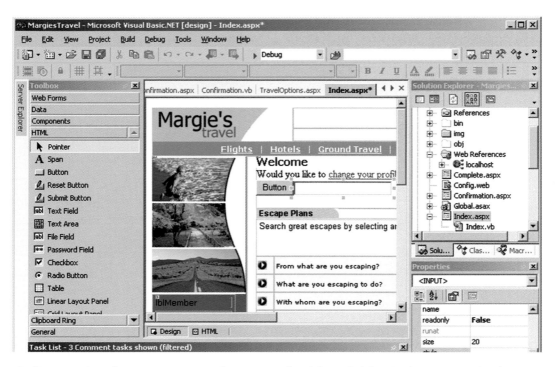

Software developers use Visual Basic to build scalable Web sites and other applications. Its design enables developers working in different locations to collaborate on creating Web applications.

C and Other Languages

C and C++ are much older computer languages that control more advanced programming. C is more complex than Visual Basic, but it is much more flexible. C++, developed by Bjarne Stroustrup, is an extension to C, adding, among other things, object-oriented capabilities. One of the wonderful things about C and C++ is that nobody owns these languages, which means that you can program nearly any operation once you understand it. Although it is possible to write code that can run on multiple operating systems, it is very difficult to do so. Instead, you will find that portions of code, or code libraries, are shared among different operating systems. These code libraries are usually tied together with specific code that cannot be ported to other operating systems. This is not the case, of course, when you are writing code for Windows.

Java is one of the newest and most popular languages. It was created by Sun Microsystems and then licensed to other companies, such as IBM. Java is similar to C++ because it offers many object-oriented capabilities, but the language itself, unlike C++, is not burdened with the history of C.

Java is primarily an Internet language. It is different than C and C++ in that it is an interpreted language. (Interpreted language can run on any machine or operating system that has the proper interpreter.) For instance, when you write Java code, the compiler gathers a language that is not specific to any particular machine. It is instead deciphered by an interpreter built for a specific machine, such as IBM. Because of this flexibility, Java is the first language that can be effectively used for the Internet, allowing client machines to run more complex code that isn't specific to each client's operating system.

Finally, assembler language is one of the lowest level languages. Growing less common by the minute because of the amount of work needed to write meaningful code, assembler language is virtually the "literal" language that every computer understands. When you write a program in C, C++, Visual Basic, or any other language (except interpreted languages), the compiler changes your code into assembler language so that the computer can understand it.

Assembler language, although cumbersome to learn, is an advantage to have on your résumé. If you know assembler language, you know how a computer thinks and works, which is not something that every developer understands. Therefore, having specific knowledge about assembler language makes you a very valuable developer.

These computer languages are only some of the more common ones available. Others include Powerbuilder, SmallTalk, Delphi, C#, PL1, Fortran, Cobol, VBScript, VBA, JavaScript, and JScript.

The most infamous person in the computer arena is Kevin Mitnick, who is known not for his programming skills or his computer language developments but for being the most famous computer hacker in the world. (A computer hacker is a person who illegally accesses another computer or computer network and manipulates or steals information from its hard drive.) Mitnick stated that he was never a hacker for publicity or personal gain. He hoarded all the information that he stole; he never sold it and would not share it with anyone.

Mitnick has been in prison for more than four years and was charged with copying proprietary software belonging to major companies including Motorola, Nokia, and Sun. By sentencing Mitnick so severely, the government was sending a message to other computer hackers. *New York Times* reporter John Markoff portrayed Mitnick as a "super-hacker who could ruin many lives if not caught by the federal government."

On January 20, 2003, Mitnick will be conditionally released. He will be prohibited from using a computer, or from acting as consultant or advisor in any computer-related matters.

SOFTWARE SECURITY

Among the greatest challenges for any experienced developer is to program his or her software with the best possible security features. While this is an important aspect of any program, it is especially important if you are developing e-commerce software. This is because customers are wary of submitting private information, such as credit card numbers, if they are uncertain whether that information will be security-protected. Normally, software can be programmed to encrypt, or scramble, data while it is being transported over public telephone lines. But, as with all software functions, a computer must be programmed to control the data that it stores.

Yet another security problem for every e-commerce software developer to consider is the program's ability to keep others from hacking into its operating system. Hacking means breaking into a computer system to manipulate or steal information. A person who does this is called a hacker. Kevin Mitnick, one of the most notorious computer hackers, explained, "People forget and grow complacent in their use of programs. This is dangerous because hackers search for the weakest link in the security chain." He continued by saying, "No one is immune to attack [by a hacker]. The most you can do is minimize your risk to an acceptable level."

Careers in Software Development

There are many career paths that you can choose in the field of software development. Depending on your entry-level skills, you might have your choice of several different positions. Many require some college education, while others require a bachelor's degree in computer science. For nearly every job listed here there is also an entry-level position in the same department that requires only minimal experience. In any case, the average annual salary for most developer positions range from $45,180 to $151,995. These figures reflect typical annual salaries (including bonuses) that are earned by developers living in urban areas.

CLIENT/SERVER PROGRAMMER

For the position of client/server programmer, there are three different levels: programmer I, II, and III.

These positions share common duties that normally include reviewing, analyzing, and modifying different types of programming systems. Usually, a client/server programmer position includes encoding, testing, debugging, and installing software to support different applications. For client/server programmers II and III, the programmer must have familiarity with database and client-server concepts and how they relate to each other, and a degree of creativity. The differences among these programmers are most evident in the level of education and experience needed to fulfill each position.

APPLICATION SOFTWARE ENGINEER

All software engineers are responsible for designing, developing, and writing software applications. They are also responsible for providing technical support and installing new software. Finally, the software engineer participates in the final testing of new products.

For this category of employment there are three different levels to achieve. The different positions are software engineer I, II, and III. In all positions there is a similarity of tasks, but some responsibilities change as you reach higher levels of employment. As your position reaches new heights you will be expected to be more creative, more involved, and more knowledgeable.

WEB SOFTWARE DEVELOPER

In most companies there are only two types of job openings for Web software developers: entry-level and senior-level positions. Entry-level employees design, develop, and implement software packages for Web sites. They are also responsible for troubleshooting, debugging, and implementing software code. Usually, positions such as these require a bachelor's degree and at least two years of related experience. Developers working at this level must also have knowledge of standard computer languages such as SQL, C++, HTML, CGI, and JavaScript.

Senior-level Web software developers consult with clients and other project team members to design, assemble, and manage Web sites. They also develop Web site installation programs. As in the entry-level position, a bachelor's degree may be required. Three to five years of experience are usually necessary for a senior-level position.

APPLICATION SYSTEMS ANALYST

Application systems analysts also gain job experience in three tiers. As with many developer positions, there is a high degree of similarity among job titles. For instance, all application systems analysts are responsible for analyzing and modifying programming systems. This is done by testing, debugging, and installing software to support different applications. A person in this position is also responsible for consulting with clients. Level II and level III application systems analysts must be familiar with relational databases (information that is stored in tables, or fields) and writing manuals describing installation processes. And, as in all higher positions, creativity and responsibility are required.

DATA ARCHITECT

Data architects design and build relational databases, which are columns or fields of stored. Each field represents one separate record. (Since the fields

Project leaders must often analyze a great deal of data before planning an effective software programming strategy.

interrelate, the computer can be programmed to perform different functions that extract answers from the saved data.) Besides creating relational databases, data architects are responsible for developing different strategies for acquiring data, archiving recovery, and implementing databases. They are also responsible for removing and deleting the database's older information on a regular basis. Usually, a data architect also designs and develops Oracle as well as multidimensional databases.

PROJECT LEADER

In this position there are three different categories of project leaders: application systems, software, and business systems. In the applications project leader position, an individual designs, plans, and coordinates work teams and is responsible for handling complex application components. He or she is also accountable for managing application systems analysts.

A project leader for software engineers is similar to the project leader for application systems. He or she also designs, plans, and coordinates work teams. The business systems project leader investigates, analyzes, and implements cost-effective solutions to business issues and computer systems. He or she is also available as technical support for team members.

SOFTWARE ENGINEER MANAGER

The software engineer manager is responsible for managing a team that designs and creates different software products. He or she is accountable for writing the product specifications (a plan or proposal), implementing and tracking deadlines, and negotiating feature sets. The manager needs to have a working knowledge of e-commerce, customer relations, and data warehousing.

Big Shots

The turn of the century has brought about many new advances in computer technology. Until recently, the only name that anyone recognized in connection with that technology was Bill Gates, the creator of Microsoft Windows. Now there are many computer programmers and developers who are equally impressive. The following five developers exemplify specific characteristics that have made each one of them outstanding in his own right.

PIERRE OMIDYAR: THE CREATOR OF EBAY

By now nearly everyone has heard of eBay (www.ebay.com), the famous electronic auction house that allows users to bid on everything from vintage toys and collectibles to electronics and automobiles.

EBay was created by Pierre Omidyar, a Silicon Valley software developer whose wife's interest in Pez collecting prompted him to think of a method to connect people who have similar trading interests. The model was simple enough: create a standard through which anyone who was registered with the company could buy and sell products in an auctioning process. Now, less than six years later, eBay boasts more than eight million users, and a per share stock price that increased by 108 percent in the last quarter of 2000.

Pierre Omidyar of eBay

EBay was developed with Oracle software, and in the span of six years has acquired other auction houses such as Butterfield & Butterfield, a company that handled expensive, exclusive merchandise, and Cruise, an online merchant of automobiles. Now, eBay's daily 1.4 million users can bid on almost anything, and the site itself has become one of the Internet's most fascinating success stories.

SHAWN FANNING: THE CREATOR OF NAPSTER

Shawn Fanning, a nineteen-year-old from Brockton, Massachusetts, had a rough childhood. His only financial support was provided by his uncle, John, who bought Shawn his first computer when he was a high school sophomore. Then, during summer vacations, Shawn worked for his uncle's online gaming company, NetGames. It was there that Shawn began to learn computer programming. When Shawn began college at Northeastern University in 1998, he soon became bored and began to work on Napster software in his uncle's office.

The main function of Napster software is to allow music to be distributed by enabling individuals to share each other's personal music collections. This created a bigger idea: peer-to-peer computing (a way of sharing information by connecting an individual's computer to a global information index that anyone can use). In May 1999, before the final text version of Napster was finished, Shawn's uncle incorporated the company and Shawn received a 30 percent share. On June 1, 1999, Napster went live (became a searchable Internet Web site, www.napster.com), and began allowing people to download the free software that enabled the swapping of music.

Shawn and John Fanning encountered controversy regarding their creation of Napster. On December 7, 1999, the Recording Industry Association of America (RIAA) sued the company for copyright infringement, asking for damages of $100,000 each time a song is copied. On April 13, 2000, the rock band Metallica also sued Napster for copyright infringement. Then, in June, the RIAA filed a motion for a preliminary injunction to block all major-label music content from being traded through Napster. Finally, on July 26, 2000, a U.S. district judge ruled in favor of the RIAA, and ordered Napster to stop allowing copyrighted material to be swapped over its network. But, on July 28, 2000, the Ninth U.S. Circuit Court of Appeals ruled that Napster should be allowed to continue operating.

Shawn Fanning

Today, Napster does not generate any revenue. This may change if the company works out a deal with the recording industry by charging a monthly subscription fee. If so, both Napster and the record companies will be paid a fee every time a song is copied. Although Shawn is still the public face of Napster, today he owns only 10 percent of the company and is not involved in its business decisions.

JAMES GOSLING: THE CREATOR OF JAVA

James Gosling is responsible for creating a break-through in computer language programming called Java. Gosling was born in Canada and was one of three children. After earning a Ph.D. from Carnegie Mellon University, Gosling went to work on "The

Green Project," a secret mission developed for Sun Microsystems. Gosling realized that in order for the tools to work, he needed to develop an entirely new computer language. He called that new language Java.

The headquarters of Sun Microsystems, Inc.

Gosling sees Java as the "concrete and nails" that people use to build an incredible network system. Today, Java is becoming one of the premiere software designs that are merging business and technology. Gosling's main goal is to support those who are using the technology by providing a language that performs, is reliable, and does all the things that generalists would like it to do.

LINUS TORVALDS: THE CREATOR OF LINUX

Another programming language that is becoming popular is Linux. Linus Torvalds, a native of Finland, created Linux after tinkering with an experimental version of the UNIX operating system on his computer when he was twenty-one years old. He mentioned the program to an Internet newsgroup and they offered him space to post it on a

Linus Torvalds

university's server. A few people downloaded the program and set to work on it, and then sent the changes back to Torvalds. Someone dubbed it Linux ("Linn-uks").

Within a year, Torvalds's software had taken on new life. Now an estimated 7 million people around the world are using computers and networks run by Torvalds's creation. Today, when Torvalds is not hacking (manipulating) Linux, he is busy working on a secret mission for Transmeta.

JERRY YANG: THE CREATOR OF YAHOO!

Another icon in the computer industry is Jerry Yang. He is one of the founders and creators of the Internet portal Yahoo! (www.yahoo.com). Yang was born in Taipei, Taiwan, and earned both his

Jerry Yang of Yahoo!

bachelor's and master's degrees in four years from Stanford University. He was only a few months away from getting his doctorate in electrical engineering when he created Yahoo! with his partner, David Filo.

In April 1994, Yang began to index favorite places on the Web for his amusement. Yang and Filo then decided to combine their indexes for other Web users. Netscape's Marc Andreessen and Sequoia Capital provided the startup fees for Yahoo!, headquartered in Mountain View, California, and the site quickly became popular.

In August 1995, Yahoo! became a business and within a year it went public, selling stock for the first time. Shares opened at $13 and closed at $33, which gave the company $848 million with which to maintain its services.

Education, Training, and Getting Started

E ducation plays an important role in your decision to become a software developer. Any computer classes that you may take during high school will help you learn useful computer skills, especially subjects geared toward constructing Web pages or learning basic programming techniques. Your career choice will help dictate what topics and skills you need to learn. To understand these skills, you have to take an active role in your education from the beginning.

HIGH SCHOOL

Today, nearly every high school offers computer classes. Some are designed to teach you how to operate a computer, while others will teach you how to program them. Take as many computer classes as you can. Some high schools now offer classes in Pascal, C, or Visual Basic.

Once you know how to use a computer, you may decide to learn how to program one. Start with the basics: Learn the fundamental principles of programming, regardless of the language. You also should learn what branches are and what conditional statements do.

After you begin learning how to program, the most important thing to do is to write programs. Write small programs that change the color of the screen, make sounds, add numbers, or print text. (Don't feel discouraged because you can't write a computer game within a week!) The more you program, the more you will learn. Then, one day, you will be able to write that game that you always dreamed about.

Once you know that you will be working with computers, learn how to type. The speed at which you type can restrict the speed at which you work. Many programmers know only how to type with the "hunt-and-peck" method, using only two or three fingers. Knowing how to type fifty or sixty words per minute is invaluable for programmers, and high school is the best place to learn this skill.

Most universities and technical colleges have computers that you can use to learn how to develop software if you don't have one at home.

COLLEGE

Typically, colleges have higher-end computers than high schools. Colleges will teach you more advanced concepts such as how an operating system works, how a compiler works, and how a database works.

College-level classes are more demanding than high school classes, so you should start your basic computer education now. Like most concepts you might study, computer basics are the solid foundation that will help you learn difficult programming skills later.

While in college, you will build a compiler, write source code, and be graded on its effectiveness. These experiences will give you tremendous confidence once you have completed them. Not every developer in today's workforce can say that he or she has written a compiler. In fact, very few can.

TECHNICAL SCHOOLS

College isn't for everybody. Fortunately, if you are interested in a future career as a software developer, there are alternatives. Today, there are many accredited technical schools that can teach you what you need to learn. After all, to become a successful computer developer, you don't necessarily need the other subjects, such as literature or history, that colleges offer.

If you cannot go to college, or if you already have a degree in a different field, consider going to a technical school. A technical school can teach you how to program in a short period of time. Unlike a college atmosphere, technical school will also put you in an environment that resembles an actual workplace. This experience teaches every aspect of the career from how to deal with clients to how to conduct a weekly status meeting. This type of learning will help you prepare yourself for the professional world of software development.

CERTIFICATION CLASSES

Certification classes are helpful for learning software development, Web development, the usage of an application, or the configuration of a machine. When you decide to take a certification class, and later the certification exam, there are two things to keep in mind.

First, the company that is certifying you means a great deal. For instance, being certified by Microsoft, Sun, or Oracle on methods to develop and use its products will take you much farther than being certified by XYZ Corporation for learning Microsoft, Sun, or Oracle's products.

Secondly, certification classes are very difficult. Unless you are already an expert in a particular field, you will probably find a certification class and test extremely challenging. These classes usually condense a wealth of information into a short time period, followed by a certification test. It is important that you pay close attention if you want to successfully comprehend the material you are learning. If not, your chances of becoming certified are slim.

INTERNSHIPS

Getting an internship is a wise idea for high school or college students. An internship means that you work for little or no money to get your foot in the door of an established company of your choice.

It is possible to land internships for software testing and software development. There are certain resources devoted to finding computer-related internships on the Web, such as Tech Teens (www.behealthylifestyles.com), or you can go directly to the Web sites of the companies that interest you, such as Oracle (www.oracle.com), Microsoft (www.microsoft.com), Dell Computers (www.dell.com), or IBM (ww.ibm.com).

Other methods of finding internships include visiting your campus career center, checking out your local or university library, reading the classified advertisements or online databases, or consulting with professionals in your field of interest.

SELF-STUDY

Probably the single most important way of learning how to develop software is teaching yourself. If you really have a desire to be a software developer, you should read books on the subject. Chat with others who have programming skills, or are already employed as programmers. Program what interests you. The more programming experience you have, the more you will grow as a developer. Understand the fundamental principles of software development and the different techniques that you can use to create applications. Subscribe to magazines and read articles about programming. The days of being called a computer nerd are over!

BUILDING YOUR RÉSUMÉ

There are a number of things that you can do now to help build a strong résumé. Even though you are not ready to get a full-time job as a computer programmer, you should practice writing a résumé. Your résumé is an important tool for telling your prospective employer about your experiences and what you have to offer at a prospective job.

A Sample Résumé

Most people will tell you that your résumé shouldn't be more than one page long. However, many software developers use two or three pages because they normally elaborate about each type of software they have developed, and the type of programming skills in which they are experienced.

Even if your résumé is just one page, it must be well composed. Quality is the key in résumé writing, especially in presentation. Be certain that there are no spelling mistakes, no incorrect URL links, and no grammatical errors. Proofread the document and check that your contact information is correct, including your telephone number and e-mail address.

You can assemble an impressive résumé even if you have never held a real job. A well-designed sample résumé of a person who is entering the workforce can be found on page 48.

WRITING FOR FUN

Most developers usually begin by writing computer programs for themselves. Write games, utilities, or anything else that comes to mind. Microsoft offers

Résumé of Robert Larson

Robert Larson
12345 Main Street
Anytown, USA
Telephone: (555) 555-1234

Shareware Experience
Calculator December 1998
Built and distributed a Windows-based scientific calculator with built-in memory functions.

Published Software Experience
Greeting Card Program July 1999
Developed a Windows-based application used to print greeting cards. Advanced features included graphic editing and print layout.

File Manager January 2000
Developed a Windows-based application that added extra functionality, such as built-in backup commands, to Windows Explorer.

Work Experience
Private Client Design May 2000
Designed and developed http://www.cleanyourpet.com.

Port Jefferson Video Store May to August 2000
Designed and developed client/server video rental system to track rentals of 10,000 videotapes.

Education
University of Albany, B.S. in computer science, 2000.

development tools for educational use that are drastically reduced in price from its full-blown corporate products. Other companies, such as Be, Inc. (makers of the BeOS operating system), give their development tools away.

Writing for fun is a great learning experience. Test everything that interests you. Don't develop programs as a chore, try to write software programs that you find fun and interesting.

After a few years of writing for yourself, you will learn computer skills that will be invaluable to your future as a software developer. Add these experiences and skills to your résumé. The fact that you created your own programs says a great deal about you and your interests. You should add a section to your résumé entitled Programs, where you list the names that you have given your own development projects, explaining what you did for each. What this information illustrates is that you enjoy what you do, and that you work well independently.

DEVELOPING SHAREWARE

After you have written a little for fun, try writing something that other people can use. For instance, write a text editor or a file management utility. Have

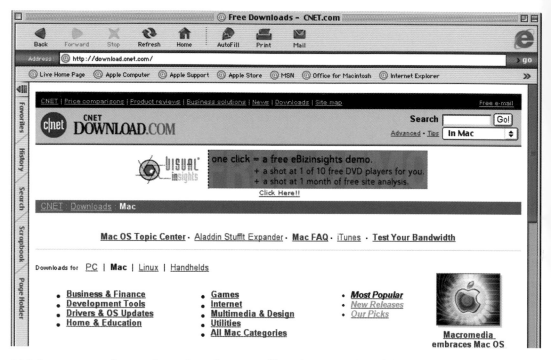

Web sites such as download.com offer thousands of free shareware files and software demos that anyone can use.

you started to write a game, but never finished it? Well, now is the perfect time to complete the task!

If your software is complete, and it performs a function, give it to others as shareware. Shareware is inexpensive software that is available to download. A very popular place to promote your shareware is at download.com (www.download.com), hosted by C-NET. This Web site has thousands of programs that can be downloaded and used by anyone. Some are shareware, while others are free demos that will work only for a limited time.

Before you think about selling the software that
you have created, first try offering it away as shareware. This will help you learn how people react to
your product. You can see how many people have
downloaded your shareware, for instance, or you can
ask them to make comments on your program. Even
if you have only one shareware product to your credit,
put another section on your résumé called Shareware,
and list the software you have created with a short
description of its function.

SELLING YOUR SOFTWARE

If you are ambitious and feel that your software can
be sold, then give selling a try. You can easily attempt
to make money with your shareware by asking people
to register it for a nominal fee, such as $10. By doing
this, you don't require people to pay for your product,
but instead, you ask them to pay a fee if they enjoy it
and use it often.

And, although you may think that no one would
pay for something that they could get for free, you're
incorrect. More people than you would expect pay
small fees for downloading software.

If the honor system isn't for you, try a resource
such as RegNet (www.reg.net) that will allow you to

Gene Kan's Gnutella search program is an easy-to-use, open environment that enables software developers to share information and instantly connect with material that is available at no cost.

sell your shareware and pay you for it. A few options are available if you want to protect your software program. You could add functionality to your programs (so that a key is required to run it after thirty days) or write multiple versions, one as a crippled demo (in which some functionality is missing) for the free version, and the other as the complete version.

Selling software is something you should consider after you have written several programs for yourself and have given several away through shareware resources. Usually, developers never sell their first program. If you have sold software, or even if you are attempting to sell a software product, put a section on your résumé called Published Software, and list the products that you have sold with a description of each one.

IN CONCLUSION

There are limitless opportunities available for individuals who have an interest in computer programming, especially in the development of e-commerce software. According to industry professionals, e-commerce is creating a revolution in business that is going to require rapid innovations in software development. Online spending reached $145 billion in 1999, and is projected to reach more than $7 trillion by 2004. That said, each new method of doing business online requires better, more efficient, and more secure software that is developed and updated by professional programmers. Consider yourself a potential programmer who has the ability not only to embrace technology, but to empower it.

Glossary

assembler   A type of program that translates a programming language into simple instructions that are understood directly by the computer.

BASIC (Beginner's All-Purpose Symbolic Instruction Code)   A programming language developed in 1963 by John G. Kemeny and Thomas E. Kurtz.

bug   An error in a computer program.

byte   A basic unit of data that is usually eight bits.

code (aka source code)   Instructions that make up a computer program.

compiler   A program that translates a high-level computer programming language into machine language.

data   Information stored in your program.

database An organized set of information. Internet search engines can be considered databases.

debugger Software that helps a developer or programmer find errors in a program.

editor A software program for editing program code.

Intranet A private network within an organization where only those who belong to that organization can read and offer data over connected computers.

Java A special programming language used primarily for the Internet and other distributed networks. Java is popular because it handles graphics and animations well.

key A string of information that is used to encode or decode computer software.

Linux An operating system developed in 1990 by Finnish college student Linus Torvalds. Linux supports many free software programs and works well with small Internet servers.

machine code Source code that is translated into a language that computers can read.

object-oriented programming (OOP) Blocks of object-oriented code that are attached in different ways to build different programs.

ported Transferred and translated from one computer to another.

programming Writing a program in a programming language.

shareware Software that is inexpensive or free and available to download from the Internet.

Visual Basic A newer, easier programming language than C or C++ that makes it possible to create working Windows programs in very little time.

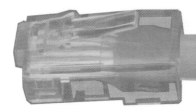

For More Information

IN THE UNITED STATES

The Center for Software Development
The SD Forum
111 West Saint John Avenue, Suite 200
San Jose, CA 95113
(408) 494-8378
e-mail: info@sdforum.org
Web site: http://www.center.org

The Software & Information
Industry Association
1730 M Street NW, Suite 700
Washington, DC 20036-4510
(202) 452-1600
Web site: http://www.spa.org

Software Patent Information
9225 Indian Creek Parkway, Suite 1100
Overland Park, KS 66210-2009
(913) 451-3355
e-mail: spi@spi.org
Web site: http://www.spi.org

IN CANADA

The Linux Professional Institute
78 Leander Street
Brampton, ON L65 3M7
(905) 874-4822
e-mail: info@lpi.org

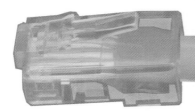

For Further Reading

Khalid, Shahid F. *Lab Windows/CVI Programming for Beginners* (with CD-ROM). New York: Prentice Hall Press, 2000.

Liberty, Jesse. *The Complete Idiot's Guide to a Career in Computer Programming*. Indianapolis, IN: Alpha Books, 1999.

Vermeulen, Al, ed. *The Elements of Java Style*. New York: Cambridge University Press, 2000.

MAGAZINES

Microsoft Development
http://www.msdn.microsoft.com

PC Magazine
http://www.zdnet.com/pcmag

PC World
http://www.pcworld.com

Visual Basic Programmers Journal
http://www.vbpj.com

OTHER RESOURCES

Shareware

TextPad
http://www.textpad.com

WinRAR
http://www.rarsoft.com

WinZIP
http://www.winzip.com

Shareware Software

Active-X.com
http://www.active-x.com

CNET Builder.com
http://www.builder.com

CNET Download.com
http://www.download.com

Developer's Resources

Microsoft's Most Valuable Professionals
http://www.mvps.org

vbAccelerator
http://www.vbaccelerator.com

Operating System Companies

Apple
http://www.apple.com

BeOS
http://www.be.com

Linux (Red Hat)
http://www.redhat.com

Microsoft
http://www.microsoft.com

Sun
http://www.sun.com

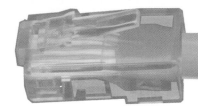

Index

ABOUT THE AUTHOR

Jason T. Roff is also the author of three database development books, including *ADO: The Definitive Guide*. He specializes in Visual Basic, ASP, and SQL server development and architecture. Jason graduated from the University of Albany with degrees in computer science and applied mathematics. He currently manages software development teams to create both Web and Windows-based applications.

Kimberly A. Roff graduated from the University at Albany with a bachelor's degree in criminal justice and sociology. She is currently getting her master's degree in teaching from Stony Brook University.

PHOTO CREDITS

Pp. 5, 24, 30, 33, 35, 36, 37, 38, 52 © AP World Wide Photo; p. 10 © Stephen Simpson/FPG; p. 18 © AP/*News & Observer*; p. 21 © Microsoft screen shot reprinted by permission from Microsoft Corp.; p. 42 © AP/*The Tribune*; p. 50 © Download.com.

SERIES DESIGN AND LAYOUT

Les Kanturek